THIS BOOK BELONGS TO:

_____

Dedicated to the knowledge seekers.

All rights reserved.
No part of this book may be reproduced in any form or by any means, electronic or mechanical, and no photocopying or recording, unless you have written permission from the author.

ISBN 978-1-958985-47-2

Text copyright © 2025 by Mimi Jones

www.joeysavestheday.com

A Mimi Book

Saint Patrick's Day is celebrated on March 17th.

It honors Saint Patrick, the patron saint of Ireland.

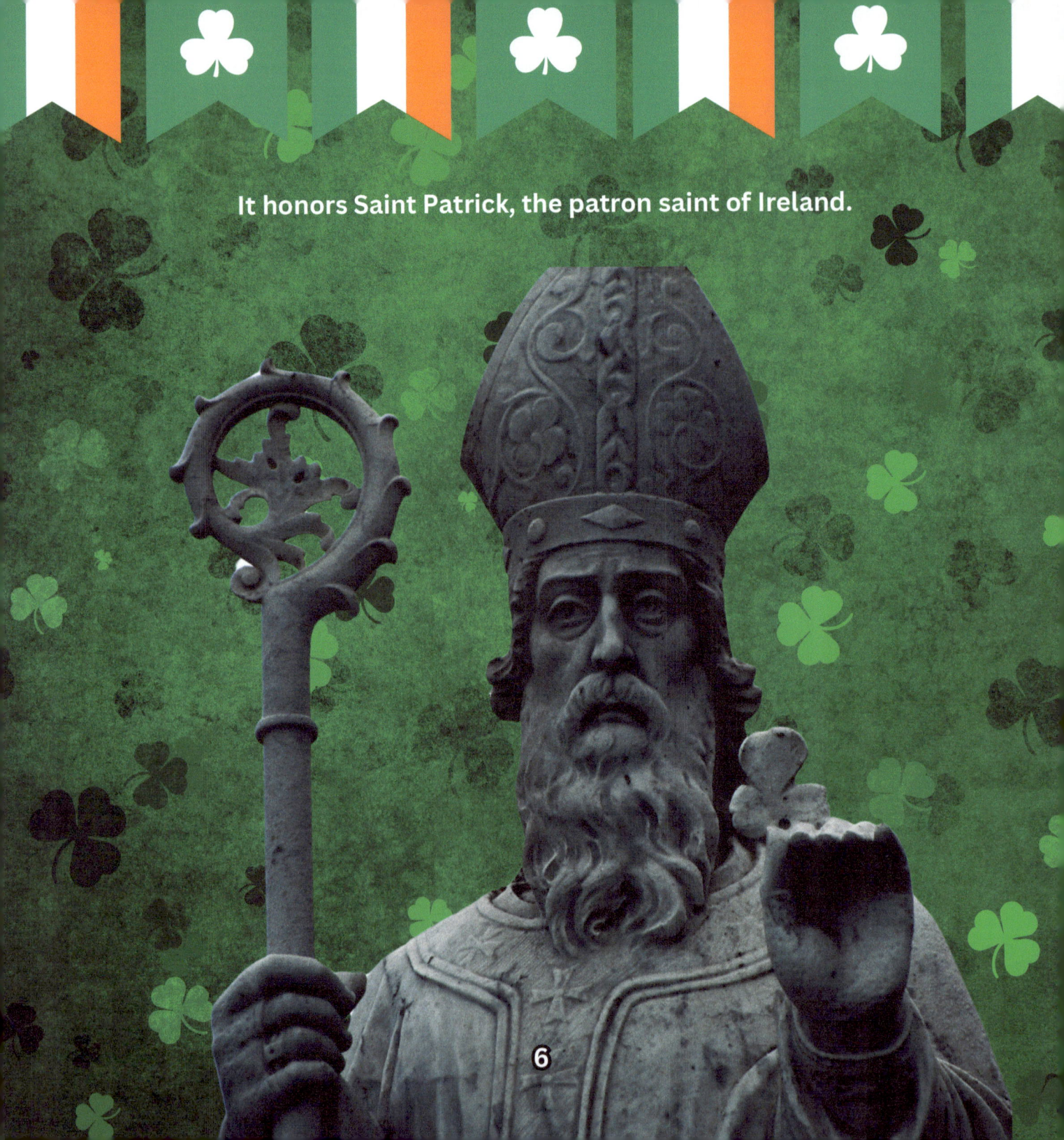

Saint Patrick was born in Roman Britain around the year 385.

MISSING

He was kidnapped and brought to Ireland as a slave at the age of 16.

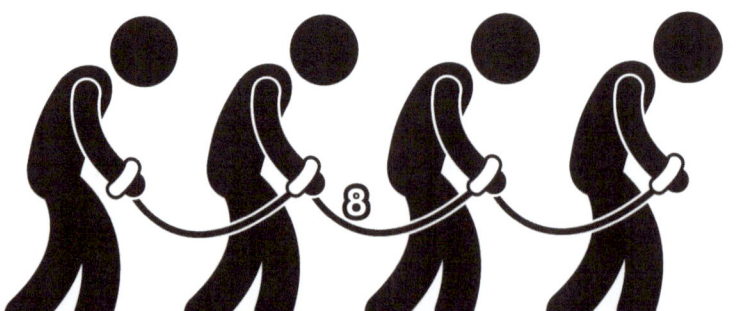

He escaped after six years but later returned to Ireland to spread Christianity.

ESCAPE

The shamrock is a symbol of Saint Patrick's Day because Saint Patrick used it to explain the Holy Trinity.

The color green is associated with the holiday because of Ireland's nickname, the "Emerald Isle".

The first Saint Patrick's Day parade was held in New York City in 1762.

HAPPY ST. PATRICK'S DAY

Leprechauns are a common symbol of Saint Patrick's Day, known for being mischievous little fairies.

The traditional dish for Saint Patrick's Day is corned beef and cabbage.

Dublin, Ireland, hosts one of the world's biggest Saint Patrick's Day parades.

St. Patrick's Day

River Shannon in Ireland is dyed green to celebrate the holiday.

March

Four-leaf clovers are considered lucky and are often associated with Saint Patrick's Day.

Irish dancing is a popular activity during the celebrations.

Saint Patrick is said to have driven all the snakes out of Ireland.

The Irish flag has three colors: green, white, and orange.

Leprechauns are said to hide their pot of gold at the end of a rainbow.

Let's Celebrate

Saint Patrick's Day is celebrated with festivals, parades, and parties.

HAPPY ST. PATRICK'S DAY

Saint Patrick's Day is a public holiday in Ireland.

"Danny Boy" is a famous Irish song often sung on Saint Patrick's Day.

Green attire is worn to avoid getting playfully pinched.

The Claddagh ring is a traditional Irish ring given as a token of love.

Saint Patrick's Cathedral in Dublin is the largest church in Ireland and is named after the saint.

Can you name these?